What should have been kept hidden from you

REINCARNATION

Life's Gift of Grace
Where does the journey of my soul go?

What should have been kept
hidden from you

REINCARNATION

Life's Gift of Grace

Where does the journey
of my soul go?

THE WORD
THE UNIVERSAL SPIRIT

First Edition, 2010
Published by:
© Universal Life
The Inner Religion
PO Box 3549
Woodbridge, CT 06525
U S A

Licensed edition
translated from the original German title:
Reinkarnation. Eine Gnadengabe des Lebens.
Wohin geht die Reise meiner Seele?"
Order No. S380en

From the Universal Life Series
with the consent of
© Verlag DAS WORT GmbH
im Universellen Leben
Max-Braun-Str. 2
97828 Marktheidenfeld/Altfeld, Germany

The German edition is the work of reference for all
questions regarding the meaning of the contents

All rights reserved

ISBN: 978-1-890841-64-5

Cover Photo: © Manul-fotolia.com (No. 5714171)

Table of Contents

Introduction 7
The Life I Chose Myself 11
Where do we come from? Where are we going? ... 13
Reincarnation – knowledge as old as mankind itself 14
The falsification of the Bible and its consequences 16
Reincarnation in the Bible 19
The anathemas against Origen 21
The consequences of the denial of reincarnation ... 24
Reincarnation –"automatism"? 29
The Spirit of God dwells in each person 30
Nature gives us an example 32
Are we marionettes of a cruel God? 34
Where does the soul really come from? 36
Freedom means responsibility 38
The parents' responsibility 40
People do not meet each other by chance 42
God is not to blame! 44
What upsets me about my neighbor is usually in me, as well 47
Why doesn't God intervene? 50

God gives us freedom – The Church teaches "you must"	53
Where does the soul go?	55
How do we get out from under the wheel of reincarnation?	60
What did Christ bring about with His deed of redemption?	65
End Notes	72
Books in the Universal Life Series	75

Introduction

"Original Christianity – For or Against?" Under this title several Original Christians in Universal Life came together during the autumn of 2007 in a series of roundtable discussions to share viewpoints on current critical topics, such as: "Climate Disaster – Can This World Still Be Saved?" or: "Why Doesn't God Intervene?" During the course of these roundtable discussions, to which Gabriele, the prophetess and messenger of God for our time, contributed significantly, light was shed on worldly events from the viewpoint of Inner Christianity, the Inner Religion of Jesus of Nazareth, which has nothing in common with the external power plays of the church empire.

During these conversations, the question came up about whether humankind has to presently bear the consequences for something that it brought on itself. This realization is far less surprising than the fact that so few people seem to realize that their destructive or indifferent behavior toward nature and their fellowman cannot remain without consequences. The apparently widespread "devil-may-care" attitude bears witness to a fatal lack of insight into the spiritual correlations, above all, concerning the meaning of human life and its origin and goal. Here, important spiritual knowledge was kept from the people, which Jesus of Nazareth, building on the teachings of the great prophets of the Old Testament, brought to this earth.

Gabriele summarized a significant part of this knowledge in the following sentence:
And we sense that we are not from this world, but that the world is merely a transit point for each one of us, whether a beggar or a king. We sense that we come from the Kingdom of God and through Christ, through His deed of redemption, we will return to the Father's house, to our true being, as pure beings of love from God.

What happens after a person's physical death? Can a person's soul incarnate again – under which circumstances and with what goal? And how did the knowledge about life after death, about karma and reincarnation, disappear from the Christian western world? Particularly in view of the worldwide climate disaster, these fundamental questions of humankind are of existential significance – because they are decisive for our attitude not only toward our own life, but also toward the life around us.

The following text consists of the edited highlights of two roundtable discussions on the topics "Life After Death" and "Reincarnation." A continuous text developed from the contributions of the participating Original Christians, which draws the reader into a lively conversation, during the course of which all important questions are not merely touched upon but – through the wide-open consciousness of Gabriele – are uniquely deepened.

Marktheidenfeld, Germany, April 2008
Verlag DAS WORT

The Life
I Chose Myself

Before I came into this earthly life,
I was shown how I would live it.
There were troubles; there was grief,
There was misery and the burden of suffering.
There was the vice that was to seize me,
There was the delusion that captivated me.
There was the quick rage, in which I rampaged,
There was hatred, arrogance, pride and shame.

But there were also the joys of those days
Filled with light and beautiful dreams,
Where neither lamentation nor vexation exist,
And everywhere the fount of gifts flows free.
Where love gives the bliss of letting go
To the one still bound in the garment of earth.
Where the one who escaped human pain
Thinks of high spirits as a chosen one.

I was shown the bad and the good,
I was shown the fullness of my failings,
I was shown the wounds that ran with blood,
I was shown the angels' helping deed.
And as I so beheld my life to come,
I heard a being ask the question:
If I dare to live this life,
For the hour of decision was at hand.

So once more I weighed all the bad.
"This is the life I want to live,"
My answer resounded strong and decided,
And I quietly took on my new fate.
And so, I was born into this world,
So it was as I entered a new life.
I don't lament when often I'm not glad,
For I affirmed it when not yet born.

(Unknown: attributed to Hermann Hesse)

Where do we come from?
Where are we going?

Many people don't even ask this question anymore. They are satisfied with the fact that their parents procreated them and that they now have to struggle through life, without thinking much about the meaning of this life. They want to be successful and enjoy life as much as possible. Everybody has to die someday. And what comes afterward remains a mystery for most people, if they believe at all in a life after death.

Where does this indifference and deadening of the senses come from? – Were the answers from the churches to such moving questions about life so unbearable that people preferred not to know anything more about where they come from and where they are going? According to church doctrine, a person's soul comes into existence during procreation. How this soul then develops is decided during the course of a relatively short life on earth. If the child was baptized into the church, then everything seems to depend on whether it follows church doctrine as an adult and receives the sacraments given by the priests. If it doesn't, the soul is threatened with eternal damnation.

Any one who does not accept the whole of the Church's tradition, both written and unwritten – anathema sit.[1]

And according to Catholic doctrine someone who is "excommunicated" lands in the eternal fires of hell:

> ...*The Holy Roman Church, founded through the word of our Lord and Redeemer, firmly believes, confesses and proclaims that no one outside of the Catholic Church, neither pagan nor Jew, nor non-believer or one separated from the unity will take part in eternal life, but will rather fall victim to the eternal fire, which is prepared for the devil and his angels, if before his death he does not join it (the church).*[2]

And even if we don't take this incredible threat seriously, the idea that 70 or 80 years on earth should decide about all of eternity is absurd. It is just as absurd as the theory that an immortal soul is created by mortal parents.

Reincarnation – knowledge as old as mankind itself

The teaching of reincarnation is much more enlightening. The belief in rebirth is as old as mankind. According to the psychologist C. G. Jung, it belongs to the "archetypes" of human knowledge. More than half of all mankind consider the law of cause and effect and the idea that a human being can incarnate several times as a totally natural thing. These concepts can be found in all cultures – not only in the East, for example in Buddhism and Hinduism, as many people think. The so-called Christian churches condemn reincarnation as an eastern teaching, yet, the meditation techniques of eastern religions are included in their institutional practices!

This is a false claim on their part. The concept of reincarnation was part of Greek philosophy, with Pythagoras and Plato; it was present in Egypt, and throughout history there were and are great minds, writers and thinkers, who, as a matter of course, assume that we may often live on earth in order to purify ourselves. At the time of Jesus, the concept of reincarnation was also found in Jewish popular belief.

The Jewish religion scholar Shalom Ben Chorin writes:

Apparently the concept of reincarnation was a popular belief in Judaism at the time of Jesus ... So people thought Jesus was one of the old prophets who had come again (Lk. 9:8;19) In the Talmud odd notes can often be found that imply a belief in a journey of the soul or reincarnation, for instance, the remark: 'Mordecai, that is Samuel.' Here it wants to say that the Jew Mordecai, the uncle of Queen Esther, was a rebirth of the prophet Samuel. [3]

During the time of Early Christianity, in numerous scriptures passed from hand to hand, the concept of reincarnation was assumed as a matter of course.

In the "Pistis Sophia," for example, one of the apocryphal gospels, Jesus says – in connection with the return of a soul from the beyond in a human body – that the soul drinks from a "cup the drink of forgetfulness."[4]

The falsification of the Bible and its consequences

These scriptures, however, like many others, were not included in the official canon of the church Bible. Toward the end of the second century the developing church of power, which Jesus of Nazareth did not found, first began to favor certain texts over others. This process of purposeful selection came to an end only at the end of the fourth century.

In the year 383, Jerome (345-420), received from Pope Damasus I the task of compiling a unified Latin Bible text. What developed from this is the so-called Vulgata Bible, "sold" until today to gullible people who believe it to be the faultless word of God. However, for a basis Jerome had anything but a unified text. There are presently 4860 known Greek handwritten copies of the New Testament, no two of which are alike. Theologians today count circa 100,000 different versions. Jerome, who changed approximately 3500 passages in the gospels during his work, wrote to the pope at that time:

> *Is there a man ..., who will not, when he takes the volume [Bible] in hand..., break out immediately into violent language, and call me a forger and a profane person for having the audacity to add anything to the ancient books, or to make any changes or corrections therein?*[5]

But *what* did he omit and *what* did he add? And *what* did he change? We can assume that Jerome – on the one hand, under pressure from his employer, the pope, and on the other hand, striving to please the pope and advance his career in the curia – withheld much of the teachings of the Early Christians, which were widespread by the 4th century and of which he also knew. Above all, these were references to the knowledge of reincarnation and the preexistence of the soul. Jerome knew very well that reincarnation was part of the Early Christian teachings. In a letter, he wrote about the Early Christian teacher Origen (185-254), that according to his teachings, the souls of human beings *"change their bodies."*[6]

Another example of change: Jerome knew about the significance of a vegetarian diet in the life of the first Christians. This aspect was not included in the official Bible texts either, even though Jerome himself was a vegetarian and wrote:

The eating of flesh was unknown until the deluge. But after the deluge, like the quails given in the desert to the murmuring people, the poison of flesh-meat was offered to our teeth... But once Christ has come in the end of time, and Omega passed into Alpha and turned the end into the beginning we are no longer allowed ... , nor do we eat flesh...[7]

And in Book II of the same treatise, it says:
If you wish to be perfect, it is good not to drink wine, and eat flesh. If you wish to be perfect, it is better to enrich the mind than to stuff the body.[8]

The historical falsification of the Bible by the church, which found its high point in Jerome, led mankind into an abyss that, particularly today, opens up more and more. By withholding this and other ancient Early Christian knowledge, an unimaginable spiritual disaster for all living beings on this earth and for the earth itself began its calamitous course, influencing the life of us all right up to the present time. What course would history have taken if a large part of mankind had known that negative deeds could fall back on the perpetrator in this or a future life on earth, if he did not repent of them in time and ask for forgiveness! Would there have been so many wars "in the name of God" for instance, or the unscrupulous exploitation of nature, the effects of which we are experiencing today?

Reincarnation in the Bible

Despite the extensive manipulations of Biblical texts, several things have remained preserved. By reading between the lines, an attentive reader finds many an indication regarding reincarnation and the preexistence of the soul. Perhaps these passages were overlooked while omitting certain parts.

So, in the Book of Wisdom, what is described are the "perverse thoughts" that "ungodly men" have, that is, those people who turn away from God. According to this, such a "perverse thought" is the following:

For our allotted time is the passing of a shadow, and there is no return from our death, because it is sealed up and no one turns back.[9]

[This book is part of the Apocrypha and thus, not included in all Bibles.] By implication, we can deduce that a "correct" thought would be that someone can come back again after his physical death. In the same book, we can also find a clear indication of the preexistence of the soul. Solomon, the author of this part of the Bible, says of himself:

As a child I was by nature well endowed, and a good soul fell to my lot; or rather, being good, I entered an undefiled body.[10]

There are also indications of reincarnation in the New Testament. Jesus said about John the Baptist:

"He is Elijah who is to come."[11] And later *"... but I tell you that Elijah has already come, and they did not know him, but did to him whatever they pleased."*[12] Jesus asked His disciples: *"Who do men say that the Son of man is?"* And His disciples answered: *"Some say John the Baptist, others say Elijah and others Jeremiah or one of the prophets."*[13] So, as Jews, the contemporaries of Jesus assumed that a person can incarnate several times.

In the Letter of James the term "wheel of birth" is even found in the original Greek text:
The tongue is an unrighteous world among our members, staining the whole body, setting on fire the cycle of nature, and set on fire by hell.[14]

This means that if we do not curb our tongue, we set causes that could bring further incarnations. The term is a misleading translation. Different Bibles offer different translations, for example: in the Luther Bible, "the whole world" or in the German Unity Bible, "the wheel of life" or in the King James Bible, the "course of nature."

The anathemas against Origen

An example of how alive the teaching of reincarnation was in Early Christianity, before it became the victim of a conspiracy of the caste of priests, can be seen in the previously mentioned writings of the great Early Christian teacher Origen (185-254). Without doubt, he was the best-known and most significant scholar of Christian antiquity. His knowledge and life spiritually brightened the entire Mediterranean region for over three centuries.

Origen, called "the diamond," was the first to undertake a critical text comparison of the scriptures of the Old Testament and the gospel texts that were available to him, and, in addition, to compare translations in various languages. In this, and in much more, he was about 1700 years ahead of the scholasticism of his day!

Like many other Early Christians, Origen also became a victim of the persecution of Christians, which Emperor Decius imposed over all the Empire in the year 250. He died in 254 as a result of the torture he had suffered. Yet, like all Early Christians, Origen knew about reincarnation. In his commentary on the Gospel of John, Origen wrote the following:

We should also have to enquire into the distributions of the life of each soul, and as to her [the soul's] departure from this life, and whether it is possible for her to enter into a second life in a body or not, and whether that takes place at the same period, and after the same arrangement in each case, or not; and whether she enters the same body, or a different one, and if the same, whether the subject remains the same while the qualities are changed, or if both subject and qualities remain the same, and if the soul will always make use of the same body or will change it.[15]

And in his commentary on the biblical story of Jacob and Esau (Genesis: 25), he says:
... we feel that he [Jacob] was worthily beloved by God, according to the deserts of his previous life, so as to deserve to be preferred before his brother ...[16]

The preexistence of the soul was also part of the knowledge that Origen spread. Let us allow a contemporary of Origen (185-254) to speak. Bishop Cyril of Alexandria reported:
For he [Origen] said that souls exist before bodies and lapsed from holiness into evil cravings and fell away from God; for this reason He condemned them and embodied them, and they are in the flesh like in a prison.[17]

However, Origen lived at a time in which the reversal of Early Christianity into an institution of power built on external rituals and customs taken from paganism was in full swing. He was treated with intense hostility during his lifetime – and after his death, his positions became the object of bitter differences of opinion again and again, whereby even his advocates lost sight of his original statements more and more. Thus, a later translator, (from Greek into Latin) Rufinus, (345-410) admits:

I have not translated other statements by Origen that seemed to be contrary to our belief, but have skipped over them as statements added and falsified by others and added others for an illumination of what we found in other books by him said more clearly.[18]

His writings were already falsified by the end of the 4th century and were systematically destroyed by representatives of the Church.[19] What remains of his original writings today is scarce. Nevertheless, Origen's teachings were spread over much of Europe by way of Arius (c. 260-336) and Wulfila (313-383) as so-called "Aryanism." This "heresy" was a thorn in the side of the Church. It goaded the Eastern Roman Emperor Justinian into waging war, almost totally eradicating the East Goths in Italy, who had embraced Aryanism. In 543 at a synod of the Eastern Church in Constantinople, and in preparation for this war of eradication, Justinian had Origen's teachings banned, insofar as they were still known. This was done in nine martial-sounding anathemas, which ended in the sentence:

Anathema to Origen ... together with his nefarious and execrable and wicked doctrine and to whom-

soever there is who thinks thus, or defends these opinions, or in any way hereafter at any time shall presume to protect them.[20]

Reincarnation as such was not expressly mentioned in these anathemas, but they did include the preexistence of the soul and the *"restoration of all things,"* that is, the teaching that all people and souls would again be with God one day, thus teaching that there is no *"eternal damnation."* With this, they put an end to the Early Christian teaching of reincarnation. And why did this happen? Because the belief in reincarnation frees people from all dogmas and ecclesiastical laws. Ten years later, the anathemas, supplemented by six more, were reinforced at the Second Council of Constantinople in 553.

The consequences of the denial of reincarnation

With this, the truth of the heavens was officially extinguished over a longer period of time. If Jerome had included this Early Christian knowledge about reincarnation in the Bible that was contained in Origen's writings as well as in the apocryphal gospels, thus making it available to western culture, the past 1700 years would have taken a completely different course.

Mankind would be actualizing totally different, higher ethical-moral values in daily life, because the knowledge of reincarnation and of the law of sowing and reaping also implies an awareness of responsibility for one's own life and behavior. Perhaps the earth would already be a paradise and Jesus, the Christ of God, would have already made true His Kingdom of Peace that had been announced to us, because people would have lived according to His teachings and His commandments. But instead of the teachings of reincarnation and of the love of God for His children, instead of the teaching that God dwells in each one of us and is the life in all things, and that the earth is a place of probation for fallen souls – as Jesus, the Christ, taught to His disciples, and thus, to us – an external doctrine filled with blood-thirsty, stone-age sacrificial rites, and the teaching of eternal damnation and of a punishing, cruel God was proclaimed by the Church. The papacy was established, which Christ never wanted, and, with violence, with fire and sword, the falsifications in the Bible as well as the papacy were forced onto mankind.

This course, initiated by the ruling caste of priests and the worldly leaders servile to it, the nobility and the politicians, contradicts the works of the Christ of God until today, thus serving not God, but His adversaries.

The rough falsification of the truth by the Church doubtlessly shaped the awareness of the population of the western world for a long time – and via this, the awareness of a large part of mankind as a whole, practically poisoning it.

The calamity began when the caste of priests silenced the prophetic word, which was still alive in the Early Christian communities:
And we have something more sure, the prophetic word, to which you will do well to pay attention as to a lamp shining in a dark place, until the day dawns and the morning star rises in your hearts.[21]

The grab for power by the caste of priests and, with this, the reversal of Early Christianity into its opposite, would hardy have been successful, if during the previous centuries people had believed in the prophecy of the Old Covenant, the Old Testament, and if they had done what God had taught through the true prophets of the Old Testament, then later, the Church would not have had this power. But the prophets were persecuted from the very beginning, many were killed and much more was done to them. Now, you can read about them and their teachings in the books of the institutional churches, but what they taught is not lived. So the applicable question is: Does the Church teach what Jesus taught?

Quite the contrary: Jesus hangs on the cross in the churches as a corpse. This is nothing more than a mockery of Jesus, the Christ, of the One who brought us all the victory, the life, and the resurrection in each heart that turns to Him. The cross with the corpse, which was unknown to the first Christians, serves the adversary forces as a symbol for His alleged defeat.

Jesus taught love of enemy; He warned us not to accumulate the treasures of the world, which moths and rust consume; He neither appointed priests nor baptized babies. He also taught: *"And call no man your father on earth, for you have one Father, who is in heaven."* [22]

That was the teaching of Jesus, the Christ.

On the cross, Christ said: *"It is finished."* – It is done. He brought mankind the light of the Father, the power of redemption. So then, what does the Church still want? What are the sacraments for? For what purpose is the adoration of monstrances, of holy figures, the worship of relics, addressing a human being as "holy father," kissing a ring, on which so much human – and animal – blood clings? What is all this for, since Christ said: *"It is finished"*?

Here, too, are many questions: What immeasurable guilt must weigh on this Church? How many wars would never have been waged? How much suffering would nature and the animals have been spared? If the teaching of reincarnation and the insight that what a person sows comes back to him had found their way into people's hearts early on during the first centuries after Christ's path on earth

– how would the earth look today? Would we then be talking about the destruction of the planet as we are today?

But the time has come, in which the Christ of God has again given mankind the knowledge and understanding of reincarnation, in the prophetic word, given through Gabriele, the teaching prophetess and messenger of God for this time. For over 30 years, God, the Almighty, kind Father, has been speaking again to His children. And, as Jesus announced 2000 years ago, He has led us into all the truth, through the prophetic word, insofar as people can understand it.

The message of the Spirit of the Christ of God for all people living in this great turn of time, His teachings through Gabriele, contain all-encompassing answers to the fundamental questions of our existence, for instance: Do we live on earth more than once? If yes, why and what for? Where does our soul come from? What characteristics does it have when it incarnates? And where does it go when it slips out of its physical vehicle? In what condition does it then find itself? And: To where does this journey of our soul lead? What goal is it striving toward?

Reincarnation – "automatism"?

Since the concept of reincarnation understandably does not fit into the concept of church doctrine, church theologians turned belief in reincarnation into something spooky, like a specter, as it were, in order to be able to condemn this belief more easily. They say it is a "mechanism" or an "automatism," that is incompatible with the dignity of human beings and with the filiation to God. Actually, the concept of reincarnation is closely connected to the law of sowing and reaping, which the apostle Paul, who is so revered by the Church, talks about: *"Do not be deceived; God is not mocked, for whatever a man sows, that he will also reap."* [23]

Viewed the other way around: A person reaps what he himself previously sowed. What we encounter in this life is what we ourselves have caused – in this, or possibly in another life. Today, we may recognize it and clear it up with the help of the Christ of God. Isn't this a wonderful gift of grace? We can be thankful that God gives us a new chance, over and over again, to free and purge ourselves from our burdens, rather than having only one single lifetime, during which everything is supposed to be decided once and for all, as the Church claims.

The principle of reincarnation has nothing to do with "self-redemption," which would make the Nazarene's Redeemer-deed superfluous. On the contrary, the Redeemer-deed of the Christ of God is what makes us capable of standing up again with His help when we have fallen, of turning back and changing our ways from within, again and again, and gradually developing to a higher level, from incarnation to incarnation, by fulfilling His will more and more.

The Spirit of God dwells in each person

True Christianity means to be an absolutely free Christian. It means to belong to Christ, because He, Jesus of Nazareth, asked people to follow Him. To follow Him means not only to accept His teachings, but to also put them into practice in daily life. This results in an inner religion, the Inner Christianity, for the Spirit of God is within, in each person.

True Christians are aware that every person is the temple of God and that the Spirit of God dwells in him. Because the Spirit of God can be found in the very basis of our soul, Original Christians go within. They pray to within, to the Christ of God in their soul.

Why then, an outer religion, an outer Christianity? Why churches of stone, if every person is the temple of God and every person can pray directly to the Christ of God? A quiet chamber is perhaps advisable, so that we can go within and pray deeply, but a splendid church of stone is not needed for this. Jesus taught this. One of His pupils, Stephan bore witness to this: *"Yet the Most High does not dwell in houses made with hands."* [24]

In view of this, we have to ask ourselves: Why are there so many stone churches filled with countless treasures; why are there so many cathedrals and gold-trimmed so-called "houses of God"? Let us realize that God does not dwell in churches of stone; He dwells in each person.

The outer religion, the church religion, keeps a person unfree. It has rules and regulations, dogmas, rites and rituals. It is an institution of cults and rituals and not lastly, an institution that preaches that a person who doesn't fulfill the rituals and church rules is eternally damned – by God! This means he is damned to the unceasing torments of hell, to unbearable tortures, cast out into the furthest place from God. But there is no eternal damnation in the Kingdom of God. This threatening message of "eternal damnation," which amounts to a teaching of hatred, could only take possession of those believing in the Church, because the Church, by suppressing the knowledge about reincarnation, denied God's grace, as it were, and plunged human beings, His children, into the darkness of a dismal, helpless state of being lost.

When theologians now object, saying that reincarnation can be compared to "automatism" and that it does not pertain to the children of God, that is nonsense. Because we could also say that nature is a kind of automatism. We human beings come from the earth and belong to the Mother Earth, and thus, to nature. And if all the occurrences in the whole of nature were automatism, this would also apply to reincarnation. But nature is not automatism, and neither is reincarnation. Instead, it is a "natural law," which includes the freedom to further develop oneself from incarnation to incarnation and ultimately to spare oneself further incarnations.

Nature gives us an example

Let's just think of spring: The sap begins to flow from Mother Earth. The trees leaf out. Fruits begin to form. Summer brings them to ripeness. In late summer, in autumn, nature gives up the fruits. And autumn and winter are times of rest. But these processes are not automatism, but a coming, in order to develop, a withdrawal, in order to come again and to give anew. It is also similar with human beings. When the physical body dies, the soul can come again, in order to fulfill what is in the eternal law, giving and receiving – the giving of spiritual fruit and the receiving of eternal life.

But if a person has *not* fulfilled these laws of life, then the soul is even more or less willing to come again, in order to get rid of the all too human aspects, to reduce the blockage to giving and receiving, until it has learned to give from life and to receive from life, so that it can return to the eternal Father's house, step by step. This, however, has nothing to do with automatism, but is solely by the grace of God. And in this grace, there is no place for "eternal damnation," which still fascinates many church faithful. With this, eternal damnation is made void. And thus, the institution church would also be made void, which has tried to bind people's souls to itself for centuries through this threat of damnation and through the salvation-automatism of external rituals.

Anyone who does not believe in reincarnation as a Catholic or Protestant must automatically believe in eternal damnation, because if a soul is severely burdened, according to church doctrine, it is eternally damned. But not according to the grace of God! Because a soul weighed down with sin can come again, to get rid of its guilt step by step, to become free for the life, which is God – and to enter into the life, which is God, and thus, into the Father's house.

Are we marionettes of a cruel God?

Where does the soul actually come from? According to church doctrine, an immortal soul is created at the moment of procreation. But by whom?

Church doctrine assumes that God participates to a certain extent during procreation, in order to create this immortal soul. Formulated somewhat pointedly, we could say that the church turns God into man's creation-servant. When two people come together and procreate a child, then, allegedly, during this act of procreation, an immortal soul develops, because God is working with the parents.

If God were to participate in procreation, to create an immortal soul, then He, the omniscient One, would also know that later He would perhaps send this immortal soul into eternal damnation! This would be a God of vengeance!

This more or less holds true for Catholic and Protestant-Lutheran doctrine. But with Lutheran doctrine, there is something more: Luther assumed that God knows from the beginning which souls, procreated and created in this way, will land in eternal hell and which in heaven. According to Luther's teaching, a person's freedom doesn't really exist; instead, the person is predestined to live through a certain fate, which God knows from the outset. – A cruel God!

If this were actually so, then we would be nothing more than marionettes, who would have to be compliant in following what some kind of capricious God has planned for us!

According to Lutheran doctrine, God rides the human soul, as it were, and God takes away from this soul the freedom to make an independent decision, as He is in total possession of this soul. For this reason, we can conclude that Lutheran doctrine denies freedom, and actually, isn't even compatible with the German constitution, as well as all other constitutions based on freedom. Because when human freedom is denied, so is the freedom to decide between good and bad, to follow the laws of God and the laws of people, or not to follow them.

If this is true about Luther's teaching, then common sense dictates that we ask ourselves: Well, if God already decided everything for me, what am I going into this church for? Of course, the Lutheran pastors are also aware of this dilemma and therefore they will tend to cover it up rather than to propagate it among the faithful. After all, they have to assume that people will use the minds God gave them.

The Lutheran doctrine, in particular, is strongly influenced by the sentence of Luther, and of Paul, too, that faith alone is enough, and that it really doesn't depend on a Christianity that is put into practice in one's works. But of what use is my "correct" faith to me, if I belong to the unfortunates of mankind whom God already knows will land in hell?

Paradoxes abound! And for this, in Germany, for example, church taxes are paid so that taxpayers can land in hell and things go well for the preachers of hell?

Most German people pay their church taxes – in other places, people give their tithes – without knowing what kind of doctrine they are paying for with their tribute. And the Lutheran Church tries to more or less embellish and gloss over this crass teaching of its founder. Only a few Protestant-Lutherans know how much this teaching brought by Luther into this world actually disdains human beings with its denial of human freedom.

Where does the soul really come from?

The soul was originally an unburdened spirit being in the Kingdom of God. But then, some of the spirit beings turned away from God; they fell away and fell into the depths – figuratively speaking. And so, the Fall, a rebellion against God, developed in this way. Divine beings wanted to be omnipresent; they wanted to be like God.

But since there is only *one* God, *one* Absolute Law, which encompasses all things, basically one cannot rebel against God. The one who rebels falls into the effects of his causes, into the harvest of the seeds he has sown.

Through the Fall-event, the fallen beings became ever more compressed, from the spiritual, the fine-material, all the way to a material existence, in a coarse-material garment. In this material garment, as a human being, the soul in its physical vehicle is bound to the law of cause and effect, which ultimately it created itself. As long as the soul in its physical body is subject to these spiritual principles, it also has to make amends for the disorder, which it brought into the cosmic order through its transgressions. This is actually quite plausible and apparently just. Because a person cannot expect of God – as the theologians apparently do – to simply miraculously do away with the disorder that the individual soul has caused through all-too-human, sinful behavior. For God gave His children freedom. And this freedom, along with the law of cause and effect, requires that we have to make good again what we have caused.

If God were to simply take our sins from us, what would be gained? What would happen if, for instance, He were to make a violent person peaceful, that is, take away his guilt, what he had practiced on others, without realizing it, without feeling remorse and turning back and changing his ways? Without realizing and recognizing it himself, the person would not change; after a short time, he would do the same again, for instance, act violently. And if God were to keep the person peaceful with

His power – what would the person then be, other than a marionette?

Freedom means responsibility

At the same time, the God-given freedom means a great responsibility for our life. And both – freedom as well as responsibility – represent a threat for the Church, because it can exert less and less power over people who act freely and responsibly. As more and more people are realizing, God is a God of love and freedom and not a God of punishment.

Ultimately, each person decides himself about another incarnation of his soul or the purposeful journey home to the Father's house. This is why the Eternal One taught us the Ten Commandments through Moses. This is why His Son, Jesus, the Christ, came. He taught us God's love and the path back to the Father. In His immense love for us human beings, He brought us freedom and light. Let us go to Christ! Let us go into our temple, to pray, for each person is the temple of God. If we keep the commandments and the teachings of Jesus in our daily lives, we exclude a future incarnation. We will then no longer have to incarnate, since it is only our sins that draw us back to earth.

Often we hear: "Reincarnation? That's not Christian!" But what *is* Christian? Christian is to do what

Jesus taught us. And when we do *not* do what Jesus taught us – think of His Sermon on the Mount or God's Ten Commandments given through Moses – then this is un-Christian; it is a sin and we burden ourselves. Where does this burdening go? It goes into our soul, and the garments of our consciousness are in accordance with this.

The particles of a pure spirit body can be compared to shining, spiritual pearls. Through unlawful thinking and acting, the person causes shadows on these pearls in his soul; he transforms down their vibration.

When we pass away, the soul gradually slips out of our physical body. It takes along these burdened garments of consciousness; they are the transformed-down forces of consciousness; it is then enveloped in this fluidum, also called aura. If our soul then incarnates again, it does not radiate pure light into the body; instead, it radiates these garments into the body – the "pollutants," so to speak, of our previous incarnation. These pollutants, the burdened "pearls," then have a corresponding effect in our body. They mark us and during the further course of our life, they again shape the world of our thoughts and the design of our existence.

If we live according to the commandments of God and the teachings of Jesus, no further incarnations are necessary. And why not? Because the "pearls" are pure, since we are going homeward. God did not create reincarnation, we did, because we polluted ourselves. We burdened our heavenly particles with sinful aspects – our all-too-humanness. We dipped into the shadow realm of the human ego, instead of moving toward the light.

To repeat for clarity's sake: It is not God's will that a soul go through many incarnations. It is His will that a person cleanse his soul and body here and now, in this life on earth, to the extent that no further incarnations are necessary.

Let us remember that God did not create the wheel of reincarnation; we human beings did! God wants nothing more than to have us, His children, with Him again.

The parents' responsibility

We know from the eternal law of life that when a child is procreated, a soul draws closer from the worlds beyond. We also know that everything is energy and that like attracts like. The future parents attract a soul that fits their vibration. In the vast majority of cases, this means that child and parents have something to clear up with each other, and that's why it is a great responsibility for the parents-to-be. They should know that they attract a child that corresponds to their genes. What they have in their genetic make-up, the soul also has something similar in its particle structure. Because of this similarity, it comes exactly to those people who now become the child's parents.

It can be that in previous lives, the child was mother or father to these parents, that as family members they created causes together, which now chain them together in terms of karma. They can loosen these chains with each other, today, in this life, father, mother, child. As soon as this happens, the child may possibly go its way. And so, those involved come together first in a family, so that they may bring many a thing into order and free themselves from this guilt, cleansing the soul according to the teachings of life, so that, each one for himself, may freely continue the path to the Father's house as soon as possible. In reality, the parents and the child are nothing more than brothers and sisters – as viewed from the homeland – divine beings of unity in the Father's house.

If the parents were aware of these spiritual interrelationships, this would give them a totally new way of relating to their children and surely also make possible a very different way of bringing them up. They would then know that similarities attracted them to each other, a common task on both their parts. This would be the basis for a child-rearing concept, which for the parents, and also for the child, would be like taking a deep breath. For the parents could free themselves of what was in previous lives and so could the child. The souls would become more light-filled and the human beings freer and the decision for the next step on the path to eternity would become easier.

There is no coercion in reincarnation, but again, only the free will of the soul! The more burdened a discarnate soul is, the more it is drawn to reincarnate in a human body. The more light-filled a soul becomes in the body of a human being, the less the soul thinks about reincarnation after the death of the body. Instead, it puts all its efforts into returning to eternity, to God, as soon as possible.

People do not meet each other by chance

What applies to the relationship between parents and children can also be applied to the relationship between all people who meet each other in this incarnation on earth. Without a doubt, this is a very important aspect of reincarnation: We don't meet certain people by chance at work, at our apartment house or at a sports club. We don't quarrel with our neighbor by chance or get along well or not so well with our colleagues. It is possible that we are now meeting again, to have the opportunity to bring to a close the unfinished tasks from former incarnations. How? By taking our fellow men seriously, for instance, by listening to each other and above all, by forgiving one another.

Just by taking into account that a particular antipathy toward someone or other can't necessarily be traced to his disagreeable behavior, but may have already been inherent in me because of former antipathies, gives me the chance to make peace with my neighbor more easily and to get along with him better. The more consistently I look for my own part in these occurrences, the sooner it will become clear that over the course of time I myself basically laid the track in a former incarnation for much that I encounter here on earth. It must not be exactly the same situation, but it could be similar negative behavior patterns, with which I caused something to others that now in turn comes back to me.

Figuratively speaking, this applies to entire nations, peoples or tribes that encounter each other. Perhaps many a great historical antagonism – for example, between Islam and Christendom, since it comes up again and again over the course of history – can be traced back to ancient battles and to people who were then a part of these disputes and now oppose each other again.

The knowledge about reincarnation makes it easier for us not to all-too-quickly blame our neighbor, saying: "He's so bad and so mean." We sense that perhaps there is something that goes far beyond our momentary life.

In these modern times, since people know that no energy is lost, this could open the way for the teaching of reincarnation. And do we suddenly want to exclude this merely because of our thoughts and feelings? Should all our feelings, thoughts and actions simply disappear into nothing? The law of God does not account for this.

God is not to blame!

When we take into account that what happens to us in this life can often be traced back to the causes from a former incarnation, God appears to us in a totally different light. We will then no longer accuse Him so readily for why this or that "injustice" happens to us, and why us, of all people. Instead, we may think about whether the blow of fate that is now happening can perhaps be traced back to negative energies sent out earlier that are now coming back to us again.

If we have grasped these correlations, we will no longer accuse God. The arbitrary God, the God of vengeance, presented in church doctrine, which leads many priests to present Him as the perpetrator when large accidents occur, disappears, if we are aware that we are on earth more than once, and that which we are experiencing is a self-made fate.

However, this does not mean that we can see through the blows of fate of others or even self-righteously point at them, because they are "themselves to blame." With this, we would only be burdening ourselves again, to say nothing of the fact that no one knows what will still happen to him in this life.

The God of vengeance is the god of the churches, not the God of the universe, not the God of love. If we see God as a God of vengeance, then the church can cast its spell over us. But if we turn to the God of love, we are turning to the One who is our Father, as all Christians pray in the Lord's Prayer. Then we will never deliver ourselves up to some person or other or to a church institution. Instead, we go toward God in us, to a loving Father, or to the Redeemer, Christ, who supports us, so that we may find the way back to the Father, into the Father's house.

Something else is also good about the knowledge that we brought our fate from previous existences. Namely, we can then understand that an opportunity is being offered to us to cleanse our soul and, after this earthly existence, to return to the Father's house, that is, to the realm of light, from where our soul once went forth. The result of this is that it becomes much easier for us to accept what is happening to us.

To accept our fate – that is, not making others responsible for it – does not mean that we should become resigned and let ourselves fall before it! Fate is not written in stone; there is no such thing as a standstill in all of life. God wants us to follow His commandments and inherent laws, so that it goes *well* for us. As soon as we turn to Him and make efforts to live more and more according to His commandments, it can be that our fate will also take a turn – if it is good for our soul.

Certainly, discord occurs every now and then. We wrangle with our fate. We are human beings and we are not perfect. And even though we know that we caused the fate ourselves, we nevertheless rebel against it at first. But with the knowledge about the spiritual correlations, it somehow makes sense to us that what we now have to suffer, we can get rid of with the help of the Christ of God and can liberate our soul, in order to return to the light as a healthy, joyful, light-filled, perfect being.

The following could also bring about a spiritual change of heart: We suddenly see more deeply into things. We listen into the words of our neighbor and can help him. We smell, taste and touch with our senses, but our perception is increasingly brighter, lighter, freer. Our level of feelings opens up and we sense more and more that in us is a light-filled being, which we call soul, which breathes, which breathes ever more deeply, ever more freely, which gives us, the shell, impulses: "Remember this every day. Clear up the all-too-human aspects, the sinfulness, that the day shows you and go back to the Father's house at the hand of the Christ of God. Go with Him step by step, by doing what God wants and not what someone else wants, for example, the Church!"

This is freedom! This is the life that we should strive for. And what does life actually mean? Does that which is life have a birth itself? Does "life" have a death? Life is God, and God is eternal, and so are we, the life in God – eternally.

Life is God. And no one can take life from us, because the Christ of God is the way, the truth and the life. If He, Christ, is the life in the Almighty – who can take it from us?

What upsets me about my neighbor is usually in me, as well

We know that there is no reaction without an action. The law of cause and effect, also called the law of sowing and reaping, is based on this fact. It can happen that we are annoyed with a person, whom we may not even know. We go down the street and a passerby comes toward us. We look at him and he irritates us. What's going on here? Ten pedestrians could go by; we look at them, look them in the eye and nothing happens in us. But the eleventh one irritates us spontaneously, even though we don't know him. We disparage him or we envy him, for instance. What does the law of reincarnation say here? No reaction without action! Since there is a reaction here, an action must have taken place at some time or other.

This fellowman brought something into movement that is in us. It could be prejudice, it could be ideas or other negative thoughts, which the other ten pedestrians didn't move in us. But *why* do we get upset over the eleventh passerby? Because the energy of the day says to us: "Here comes someone with whom you should clear up something in your thoughts, what you now thought negatively about him."

This doesn't mean that we approach him and tell him this; instead, we admit to ourselves: "The energy of the day reflected something to me here. Now I have to see to it that I look more closely at what upset me so much, so that I may recognize that I am part of it myself; that in the past I had such or similar thoughts against a person – maybe not necessarily against this one who just upset me – and perhaps I even spoke or acted similarly."

Why should we not tell our neighbor that we thought negatively about him? Usually he does not know or sense our thoughts. If we speak to him about them, our words will, in turn, cause him to have thoughts that are not beneficial for him or for us. Instead, let us trust in Christ who is active in us as well as in our neighbor.

We now have the possibility to clear up the negativity in ourselves, by feeling remorse, by silently asking for forgiveness, and then striving to no longer nurture the same and like thoughts. If such thoughts come again anyway, we should think about them again. And when we step by step decrease them, our soul becomes more light-filled and we come out of the so-called wheel of reincarnation, so that we may continue our path home into more light-filled fine-material spheres.

Isn't this teaching wonderful? It is a teaching of liberation, given from the love of the Father-Mother-God to His children. How would the world look today if many people knew about this teaching and applied it in their daily lives? There would then be people with higher, with spiritual, values, with more clarity and awareness. Instead, man has become brutal and belligerent instead of peaceable. Each one thinks solely of his own concerns; few are open for their neighbor.

What we are now experiencing on this earth is the harvest of what we human beings have sown. In reality, the divine being in each of us comes from the eternal Being and from the brother-sister-hood of the great unity. But we human beings have not accepted this brother-sister relationship. Each is against every other one and each one wants to take advantage of the others.

And if we say: "I'm not against my neighbor," then we have to ask ourselves: What about our thoughts? Aren't they at least in part directed against our neighbor? Because thoughts are also energies, energy forms; they aren't "free," as is often said. Thoughts are energies that produce an engraving in the soul. And this engraving determines the course of the law of sowing and reaping. What we engrave in our soul is what we will become. And as a soul, we bring this with us again into future incarnations, until we have cleared up the all-too-human and sinful engraving. Then the spirit being comes through again, and we can take further steps back into the eternal Kingdom of God.

Why doesn't God intervene?

People often ask why God doesn't intervene? – God gave us our free will! How can He, who gave us free will, intervene in our all-too-human will, in our stubbornness, in our maliciousness, in our offences against His commandments? We want it this way! And so, He doesn't intervene. But in His grace, He gives us the possibility to draw closer to the eternal law of love, of unity and freedom, by clearing up our all-too-human aspects.

If we observe the great cosmic event, we realize that God did intervene, but not in the law of cause and effect. However, He sent His Son, who brought us redemption. And what is redemption? It is nothing more than the light in the soul, and thus, the protection of the soul, so that it doesn't fall ever deeper and doesn't dissolve, as it is taught in eastern religions.

And so, through His deed of redemption, Jesus, the Christ, brought us the protection of the soul, thus securing for us the path to the Father's house. Our soul can no longer dissolve, because the protection of the Christ of God is there, because the light of Christ is in our soul, since He will guide us back again someday, when the individual wants this.

Since Christ brought us the deed of redemption – how should eternal damnation take place? Here we recognize the ambiguity of theologians, how they say that Christ "redeemed" us of all our sins through the deed of redemption. But if all people's souls had suddenly become free through His "It is finished," that is, if they were without guilt, why then, do maliciousness, conflicts, wars, murder, manslaughter, and being against one another still exist in this world? Why? These are sins! And so, we see that Jesus, the Christ, did not simply take away our sins, as the Church claims; instead, it was and is different: He gave our souls the supporting energy necessary to keep them from dissolving, and He is present in us as light, as power, as help, so that the soul may cleanse itself and finally return to the eternal homeland as a spirit being that is pure again. – And so, this whole teaching of the Church is absurd.

On the other hand, someone who acknowledges reincarnation as truth also accepts the law of nature and the law of sowing and reaping. He knows, and we cannot make ourselves aware of this often enough, that the grace of God consists of the fact that the soul can come again, in order to clear up what it inflicted upon itself in former incarnations as a human being. Ultimately, it, the soul, has the commandments of God and the teachings of Jesus, the Christ, in order to become free, to receive again what the spirit beings bear in themselves, the giving and receiving, the movement of life.

Why does the Church deny these facts? Let us think logically: If the church institutions were to approve of reincarnation, their whole dogmatic house of cards would collapse, because reincarnation is a gift of grace from God. Reincarnation excludes the concepts of "eternal damnation" as well as a "punishing God." It is a chance for the soul to become free of its burdens.

Isn't it perhaps exactly this that the churches don't want, this becoming free that God has made possible for human beings? They want by all means to keep their power over the souls; they can, however, exercise power only over those people who do not dare to think. The dogmas and statutes of the churches confine the soul, in which the divine spark lives, in an encasement, as it were, thus preventing the child of God from turning directly to its Father. And precisely these dogmatic fences and barriers have made it possible for the Church to delete the Early Christian teaching of reincarnation.

God gives freedom –
The Church teaches you "must"

It belongs to the "basic knowledge" of mankind that God is merciful to us, that He respects our freedom, but again and again He also makes us aware of the possibility of turning to Him. However, this basic thought of freedom was denied through the statutes of the Church. A structure of fear was created in its place, and, out of fear, man turns to the alleged punishing God of the Church and not to Jesus, the Christ, who said: *"Come to Me, all who labor and are heavy laden and I will give you rest."* [25] But ultimately, the Church doesn't give anyone rest. It is solely Jesus, the Christ, who gives souls and people the way to rest with the power of life.

If we were bound by God to the rules of the Church, to the dogmas, rituals, traditions and everything else, God could rescind the Ten Commandments and the teachings of Jesus, the Christ! Because the rules of the Church would be enough. But the divine commandments and the teachings of Jesus, the Christ, do *not speak for*, but speak *against* the rules, against the traditions, against the entire doctrine of the church institutions. The Church says: "you must"; it talks about eternal damnation. On the other hand, the commandments of God say: "you shall." The teachings of Jesus, the Christ, constantly reach out a helping hand to us human beings, and we may accept it or not in complete freedom.

On the other hand, the commandments of the Church are basically not "commandments," but coercion. However, the God of freedom knows no coercion. And no trace of coercion, to say nothing of threats, can be found in the Sermon on the Mount of Jesus.

In the last analysis, the churches exclude the Ten Commandments. With their "must," they simply turn away from the commandments, away from God's hand that reaches out to us with "you shall."

Over the centuries, the true teachings of Jesus of Nazareth were darkened by the Church via the church authorities, and the scope and depth of these teachings were kept from the people. For this reason, God intervened once more. During our time, He has sent a great teaching prophet. Through Gabriele, the emissary and prophetess of God, Original Christianity has been called into life again

– and through her, a mighty Original Christian stream flows into the world, the true life in word and in the deed.

Where does the soul go?

We human beings are incarnated spirit beings. We carry in ourselves a soul, and in the depths of our soul, the divine being that comes from God. So when the physical body dies, where does the soul go?

This is a very decisive question, with which most people are totally in the dark. If we read the obituaries in the newspaper, we realize every day how much mankind is at a loss with the question: What actually happens after life on earth?

The one thinks we are immediately with God. Others think eternal rest has come, that the deceased will continue to exist without pain. Or perhaps he continues to exist only in his deeds here, and continues to live solely in the thoughts of his descendants? We simply don't know.

Through the divine prophecy of Gabriele, we learn what happens after life on earth. We merely change our aggregate state. The soul continues to live as it had lived on earth, with all its positive and negative characteristics. It takes them along and will then be faced with the question of what to do with them: whether to continue its development in the worlds of the beyond, or whether to incarnate again, and take on a new earthly existence for a quicker purification of the soul.

The worlds of the beyond, in which the souls can stay for a time, consist of partially condensed solar systems, part-material or finer-material worlds. The souls dwell in the finer-material worlds, far beyond our material cosmos. When a physical body now passes on, the soul goes to one of these purification planes, these finer-material solar systems. In accordance with its active soul envelopments, its active "soul garment," it goes as if automatically to that planet in which its wrong attitudes are stored and active. It is attracted to there, as it were.

How did these purification planes, these finer-material worlds, develop? And how did density, coarse-material matter, develop?

God is love and when the Fall began, He gave the so-called Fall-beings parts of the spiritual stars and planets to take along; these enveloped themselves accordingly. After splitting off from the eternal Being, they were Fall-worlds; back then, the density of matter did not yet exist. The rebellious beings lingered in these Fall-worlds. Messengers of light went to the Fall-beings over and over again and wanted to take them back. Many did not go back, because they still wanted to be like God, thus condensing themselves more and more. This progressive turning away from their divine heritage very gradually caused the further condensation of the stars and planets, of the coarse-material planets, of the coarse-material solar systems, all the way to earth's matter, which is the dwelling place of human beings, the base of the burdened souls.

The human being as such is nothing more than a many-layered garment of the soul, a condensation, which glitters according to the burdened soul garments. This is why people's characters are so different. The ethical-moral values of man are at the lowest level, when compared with the highest ethics of the cosmic, eternal Being.

And so, after the death of the body, the soul changes over into the spheres of the beyond. If it goes into the lowest purification planes, because it is very burdened, it is still in the wheel of reincarnation. If the soul has become more light-filled, it has grown out of the wheel of reincarnation and rises to higher planes, to the so-called planes of preparation, in order to there strive toward the Father's house, step by step.

Everyone knows that no energy is lost. Because of this, neither the energy of our positive or negative thoughts is lost, nor that of our words, our ways of acting, our whole behavior. Since energies, whether positive or negative, have their effects, we shape our soul accordingly. This energetic engraving remains in the soul, even after the demise of its physical body. The soul is enveloped with all these engravings; we call these envelopments the "garments" of the soul.

In the spheres of purification, which the soul goes to after the body passes on, the garment of order, the first soul garment, becomes active first. The disorder in us radiates and wants to be rectified. The soul is given an understanding of this "garment," this burden, again and again. The soul moves in this garment until it becomes aware that it may discard it.

Divine beings, brothers and sisters, pure spirit-brothers and sisters, teach the soul and help it take off the various garments, these differing all-too-human, sinful engravings. The more the soul cooperates, to become free of these garments in the spheres of purification, the lighter and more light-filled it becomes.

And then the soul decides: Will it continue its purification process in the purification planes? Or will it incarnate again, in order to discard the remainder of its sinful aspects, since the process may go faster on the earth? Or will it remain uncomprehending, saying: "I don't believe what is being explained here; I am drawn back to the earth"? It can go into a future incarnation, when a human body is procreated that corresponds to its inputs, its active engraving.

The soul may very well wear different garments, different burdens, but what is active draws it to the earth. For the approaching journey over the earth, a so-called matrix already exists in the material universe, which consists of the person's various inputs. This matrix already indicates the appearance and the development of the soul in the earthly existence as a human being.

This results in the fact that during our present life we may already be shaping the body and the life path of a possible future incarnation on this earth. This is particularly the case when the person does not devote himself to the purification of his soul, but instead, while in the temporal, constantly violates the law of love, of freedom, unity and brotherliness, or brotherli-sisterliness. It is namely then that this matrix develops: And so, in the material universe, a body for the next incarnation is energetically formed.

How do we get out from under the wheel of reincarnation?

How do we now get out of this cycle of dying, of being born, of a sojourn in the soul realms, of being born again, of dying again? Is there no end to it at all?

Yes, there is! What did the eternal Father give us through Moses? The Commandments. We can measure our thinking and our entire behavior against them. Does it agree with the commandments?

Then Jesus, the Christ, came and gave us the power of redemption. During His life and in His teachings, He gave us an understanding of the loving Father, so that we could learn to love, which is our true being. He taught us the Sermon on the Mount. He gave us indications for a life in the earthly existence.

The teachings of Jesus, the Christ, are the ideal guideline for our way of thinking and living in daily life. And so, we have received valuable standards in the Ten Commandments and the teachings of Jesus, the Christ. If we follow these indications step by step, our soul purifies itself.

First we have pangs of conscience, and we say, for instance: "I am constantly violating what the eternal Father taught me; I am violating His commandments. I am also acting against the teachings of Jesus, the Christ, over and over again. I am burdening my soul, which is calling: Free me!"

If we truly, and from our heart, want to become free and return to the Father's house at the hand of Jesus, the Christ, remorse develops in us. Then we ask our neighbor, whom we have harmed, for forgiveness. Or, if we were downright spiteful in our thoughts, we ask for forgiveness in our thoughts.

If we have done something that is against the life of the animals and plants, against nature, we have the obligation to ask the Creator for forgiveness, because they are His creatures. He forgives. And if we no longer do the same or similar things, our soul cleanses itself and we feel that we may fulfill the laws of life, for instance, the Ten Commandments, step by step.

A simple, but effective maxim could be: What we do not want done to us we should do neither to our neighbor nor to the animals nor to the nature kingdoms. If we act accordingly, our soul will gradually become free of its burdens. The matrixes, which we may have already created, gradually dissolve in the cosmos, and we draw ever closer to our goal, to the homeland in the light.

Here, it is again apparent what nonsense it is to speak of a "karmic automatism." Because each person determines how often he will continue to incarnate. No one is forced to subject himself to a "machinery of expiation," if he does what Jesus of Nazareth taught and what has been revived by way of the prophecy of the present time.

In the divine prophecy through Gabriele, the important topic of "reincarnation" was made clear. In the book "Cause and Development of All Illness," a Christ-revelation from the year 1986, we can read the following:

A soul can incarnate and go through many earthly lives in the human garment until, through self-recognition and actualization, and by accepting My deed of redemption, it walks the spiritual path that purges and cleanses its base ego, thus increasing the Redeemer-light effective in it. Sooner or later, every soul and every human being has to undergo the purging of the soul – either in this life on earth or in further lives or as a soul in the spheres of purification, in order to again become the conscious image of the eternal Father.[26]

And so, this means that as soon as the soul has become more light-filled and no longer tends toward reincarnation, toward the earth, it can purge itself in the spheres of purification, which stand ready in the beyond for the souls, in order to return to the Father's house step by step, to its eternal primordial existence, to its eternal primordial homeland.

Here, too, we can again recognize the hand of the Lord that reaches out to us: You "must" not reincarnate, unless you are drawn to reincarnation. If nothing else is in the soul's awareness than to become a human being again, the soul goes into the earthly garment again. But if a certain purging process has been accomplished in the soul, that is, if the soul has become more light-filled, such souls feel the pull toward earth less and less. They then say to themselves: "I can also purge, that is, cleanse, myself as a soul on a purification plane." However, on the purification planes, the purging process is far more difficult and prolonged, above all if the soul is very burdened. This is why it frequently presses toward incarnation again, because as a soul in the beyond it has to endure and suffer the sorrow and pain that it caused to others as a human being. It has to see and feel in pictures how it treated its neighbor, for example, how it brought him away from his path, how it manipulated, influenced and coerced him, perhaps even to committing murder or manslaughter. This is why Jesus, the Christ, teaches us peace.

If such aspects of guilt are active, then this draws the soul back again. But if it is largely fulfilled by a life in Christ, then as a human being it walks on the path home to the Father's house. It no longer feels the pain that it had to endure as a soul. Via the energy of the day, it recognized as a human being what it should clear up and, as a human being, cleared things up before the pain and suffering began, before an illness broke in over the person. So the soul purges itself and turns heavenward, that is, homeward, toward its origin.

May we recognize the grace of the Lord here: Via the energy of the day, we receive impulses – sometimes for months, even years, before some kind of suffering or illness breaks out – that we should repent of and clear up negative aspects, so that what is in the soul will dissolve in time and we do not hasten toward a blow of fate, but we dissolve it before it becomes visible externally. Is that not grace?

It is an optimistic teaching that gives hope and comfort. As already mentioned, Origen taught it in the third century. And at the 5th Ecumenical Council of Constantinople in the year 553, this teaching was damned and cursed. Not only was the teaching of Origen condemned – that the soul existed already before its birth – his optimism was also damned: that in the end, everything would be good, that all things return to God. By damning this, the church was able to threaten us with hell.

It was at that time that this demonic, momentous change of direction took place. And today, the Spirit of God comes and teaches humankind that the teaching of Jesus of Nazareth is a teaching of redemption from any kind of all-too-human evil, a guidance toward a way of thinking and living in the Spirit of God. He tells us that everything pure, "clean," filled with light and power, just as God created it, returns to God.

What did Christ bring about with His deed of redemption?

Why did Jesus, the Christ, die?

Through His deed of redemption, a further dissolution of all forms was prevented. This is a very decisive message, which is only now being conveyed to people again through the prophecy of our day.

Christ did not die as a sacrificial lamb for a wrathful God, as depicted by the churches. He died by being faithful to His mission from the Father, and because the people had not accepted His message. To prevent a further downward development of mankind, He made His love available to all souls and people in the form of the Redeemer-spark. Through this, He gave each person and each soul the strength to return to God in freedom. And so, He did not perform magic nor did He wash away everything that we had indebted ourselves with, but instead, with His power of redemption, He gave us the possibility to become active, by turning to Him.

The divine beings, which had gone against God, wanted the dissolution of all forms created by God, that is, the dissolution of all divine beings, heavenly nature, the home planets on which the spirit beings live. These contrary beings also wanted to bring about the dissolution of duality. Duality is the connection of two spiritual beings that live in God and, in turn, bring forth divine beings, in order to further inhabit the Kingdom of God, to build it up further, to continue to create and be active for the Kingdom of God, for the heavenly homeland. Several divine beings wanted to put an end to all this – to the order and the law of the divine universe. They wanted everything that had been created to return to the primordial stream, from which the Eternal One had created spiritual, divine, pure forms, the eternal divine law of love that had taken on form. – And *why* did they want this? They did not want to be children of God, but to be God themselves, omnipresent and creator.

And so, we could say that "original sin" is the sin of the Fall, the dissolution of forms. Jesus, the Christ, took "original sin" upon Himself, by saying: This will not happen! I dissolve this original sin, by using a part of My divine-spiritual heritage, by bringing each soul the light of the eternal homeland and enveloping it, so that it can no longer be dissolved. With this, Christ protected the homeland, the eternal Father's house, and gave every soul the path back to within, to its original divine being.

Since the "It is finished" of the Christ of God on Golgotha, the adversary of God, the demon, has lost his blasphemous game. Christ was, and is, the Savior right up to the present time. Since the Redeemer-deed of Jesus, the Christ, the divine beings and the creation-gifts of God, the divine forms of Being, given from His love, can no longer be dissolved. He used a large part of His divine heritage, which since then is in our soul as a spark of light. This spark of light protects the divine being in us, the soul.

Christ did not simply take away our sins. Instead, He helps us to recognize these sins, to repent of them, to clear them up and no longer commit them. He helps each one of us, by teaching us again and again how to keep the commandments of God, to recognize and to apply in their depths His teachings, the Sermon on the Mount, to thus become pure, to return to the origin, to the eternal homeland. The meaning of the inner religion is to follow Christ in our thinking, speaking and doing, turning to Him, the Spirit of the inner being, in prayer and establishing communication with Him. And so, inner religion, Inner Christianity, means to make use of the days as it is meant to be by the eternal Spirit, honoring God and thus, doing His will.

The prayer of unity, the Lord's Prayer, begins with the words:

Our Father, who art in heaven, hallowed is Your name. Your kingdom comes and Your will is done, on earth as it is in heaven ...

This was spoken in absolute terms by Jesus, the Christ. With this, He said to us: You will return to God through the effectiveness of the eternal Father, through His Son, through redemption.

We are all going back to the Father, from whom we went forth, because a light-filled being is in each one of us. This being will return to the Father's house. For God did not create souls; He created the being of light that is deep within the soul. The soul cleanses itself; it purges itself, and what comes to the fore more and more? The being of light emerges.

Each one of us is the temple of God. God dwells in us. The more we fulfill God's will, by fulfilling His inherent laws of life, the commandments and the teachings of Jesus, the Christ, the closer we draw to our heavenly Father, the more consistently we walk at the hand of our Redeemer – out of the wheel of reincarnation, toward the realm of light, toward God, to the One who envisioned and created us before infinite eternity!

It is very comforting for us human beings that after our life on earth – if we have followed the commandments and inherent laws of God – the soul can start its journey home, because Christ also promised this to us, according to the following:

In my Father's house are many dwelling places. If it were not so, would I have told you that I go to prepare a place for you? And if I go and prepare a place for you, I will come again and will take you to myself, that where I am you may be also.[27]

And so, the dwelling places in the homeland are standing empty; our spiritual families await us. They long for us; they long for the great cosmic unity in the Father's house. And the Father's house is the unendingly great Kingdom of God! The power of God radiates to us; this is why prophets came again and again and taught the people: *"Turn back and change your ways! Turn to God. God is love. The Father loves you. He loves His child He created!"*

He would be a cruel God, if He were to punish us or even send us into eternal damnation! But no – He is our Father, who loves us. Only *we, ourselves,* can damn ourselves, so to speak. Through what? By entering the dark realms of existence, by being far from God – through our own dark thoughts, words and deeds, which are the opposite of the law of life, of our true divine heritage, which is selfless love. But even this self-imposed darkness will never be eternal, because eternal damnation does not exist! There may be a long shadow of existence, as long as we prefer shadows. But God is light! God is love, and love is warmth – this is God, our Father! He is the Father-Mother-God. He loves us and calls us.

He sent us His Son, the Co-Regent of the heavens, to give us the part-power of the primordial power, a part of His divine heritage, so that we would have a support on the way home to eternity. And this support is Christ, our Redeemer, the light of redemption in us.

Many people are afraid to die – why? Ultimately, it is less the fear of dying as such; rather, they fear, subconsciously, their own sins. Because when the soul gradually draws out of the dying body, then it becomes clear to many a person what he has caused against his true life, against his spiritual heritage. It is in this that the fear of passing on, of dying, has its roots.

To all our fellowmen, who are our brothers and sisters, we want to say: A hold, security and help cannot be found in the external world. And especially not in the sham-Christian church institutions. Therefore, come out of the stone houses that are called churches. *You* are the temple of God! And if God shines in you, if the divine being is in you, if you are an heir to the Kingdom of God, what should you then do? Pray – and live the content of your prayers. Then what is written in your hearts will be fulfilled: You are eternal life, beheld by the eternal Father, who loves you, who calls you, who sent His Son, our divine brother, so that we learn to understand that the divine power is in us, and we, each one of us, are the temple of God. Deep in our soul is the great, divine being.

The purer we become, the more easily we will pass on when our hour has come, because we will feel that Christ takes us by the hand and leads us to the Father's house, step by step. Incarnations are over with – now, the path leads straight back to the Kingdom of God!

END NOTES

[1] *J. Neuner & H. Roos,* "The Teaching of the Catholic Church as Contained in Her Documents." Edited by K. Rahner, translated by G. Steven, from the original German, "Der Glaube der Kirche." Mercier Press, Ltd., 1967, Margin Note No. 78, p. 57. (Printed and bound in the U. S. A. by the Pauline Fathers and Brothers Society of St. Paul at Staten Island, NY).

[2] *J. Neuner & H. Roos,* "Der Glaube der Kirche in den Urkunden der Lehrverkündigung." Verlag Friedrich Pustet, Regensburg, 10th ed., 1979, Margin Note No. 381, p. 256.

[3] *Shalom Ben Chorin,* "Bruder Jesus." dtv-Taschenbuch, Munich, 1977, p. 25.

[4] *G.S.R. Mead,* translator, "Pistis Sophia." 1921, Chap. 146, p. 320. Gnostic Society Library: http://www.gnosis.org/library/pistis-sophia/ps151.htm

[5] *Jerome,* "Prefaces to Vulgate Version of New Testament: The Four Gospels." From: "Nicene and Post-Nicene Fathers, Series II, Vol. VI": http://www.ccel.org/ccel/schaff/npnf206/Page_487.html

[6] *Origen,* "De Principiis, Book I, 5:3": http://www.origenes.de/primaerliteratur/auszuege-de-principiis.htm

[7] *Jerome,* "The Principle Works of St. Jerome" (Against Jovinianus. Book I, no. 18) From: "Nicene and Post Nicene Fathers, Series II, Vol. VI": http://www.ccel.org/ccel/schaff/npnf206.vi.vi.I.html

[8] *Ibid.,* Book II, no. 6: http://www.ccel.org/ccel/schaff/npnf206.vi.vi.II.html

[19] Wis. 2:5.

[10] Wis. 8:19-20.

[11] Mt. 11:14.

[12] Mt. 17:12.

[13] Mt. 16:13f.

[14] Jas. 3:6 "The New Oxford Annotated Bible, Revised Standard Version," used here, has a note by "cycle of nature," saying, or: "wheel of birth."

[15] *Origen,* "Commentary on Gospel of John, Book VI, 7": http://www.newadvent.org/fathers/101506.htm

[16] *Origen*, "De Principiis, Book II, 9:7": http://www.newadvent.org/fathers/04122.htm

[17] *H. Bauer,* "Wiedergeburt." 2nd Ed., Fruck Verlag, Pforzheim, 1998, p. 145.

[18] *Ibid.,* p. 42.

[19] *Robert Sträuli,* "Origenes, der Diamantene." ABZ Verlag, Zürich, 1987, p. 317.

[20] *Philip Schaff and Henry Wace*, Editors, "Nicene and Post-Nicene Fathers, Series II, Vol. 14, The Seven Ecumenical Councils": http://www.ccel.org/ccel/schaff/npnf214.xii.x.html

[21] 2 Pet. 1:19.

[22] Mt. 23:9.

[23] Gal. 6:7.

[24] Acts 7:48.

[25] Mt. 11:28.

[26] "Cause and Development of All Illness." Published by Universal Life – the Inner Religion, Woodbridge, CT USA, 2008, p. 71.

[27] Jn. 14:2-3.

Books in the Universal Life Series

This Is My Word –
A and Ω – The Gospel of Jesus
The Christ Revelation,
which true Christians the world over have come to know

A book that lets you really get to know about Jesus, the Christ, about the truth of his activity and life as Jesus of Nazareth. From the contents: The falsification of the teachings of Jesus of Nazareth during the past 2000 years - Jesus loved the animals and always spoke up for them - Meaning and purpose of a life on earth - Jesus taught about marriage - God is not a wrathful God - The teaching of "eternal damnation" is a mockery of God - Life after death - Equality between men and women - The coming times and the future of mankind, and much more!

1078 pages / Order No. S 007en, ISBN: 978-1-890841-17-1

The Word of the Christ of God –
to Mankind Before this World Passes Away
Nearer to God In You

Believe, trust, hope and endure! What do these mean and how can we apply them on our way to God? How do we turn belief into an active faith? How do we develop trust? Hope is expressed in setting goals that are carried out with confidence. What does it mean to endure in the divine sense? Experience the Inner Path in condensed form. Simple clear words, given to all people who long for God and a fulfilled, happy life in freedom. A gift from God to all His human children.

112 pages / Order No. S 139en, ISBN: 978-1-890841-45-4

Where Did I Come From? Where Am I Going?

The wherefrom and whereto of our life is no longer a mystery. Following explanations on the important questions on life after death, answers are given to 75 most frequently asked questions on this topic.

75 pages / Order No. S 407en, ISBN: 978-1-890841-09-06

The Work of The Christ of God and of the Divine Wisdom
From the Love, therefore, Came the Wisdom and Dwells among the People, Today, in the Time of Redemption

According to Plato, wisdom, which is "Sophia" in Greek, means "the knowledge of divine ideas." Many high values come together in wisdom: knowledge, understanding, as well as insight and the ability to discern, also intellectual capacity and experience, as well as diligence, sagacity and good judgment. The divine Wisdom is the deed. True, divine Wisdom always begins with respect for God, and therefore, surpasses any human wisdom. Without upholding high standards, without righteousness, justice and truthfulness, there is no divine Wisdom.

Who or what is the divine Wisdom? Why was wisdom driven from theology? Who is the Comforter, who is the "exalted woman," talked about in the Bible? And why do we know so little about the prophets? - The authors extend a great bow over the work of the Christ of God and of the divine Wisdom - from the very beginning of time until today. Who presently lives and works on the earth is comprehensibly demonstrated: It is the incarnated Seraph of divine Wisdom.

Let your heart be touched by the unobtrusive perseverance and sovereign love, with which the divine Wisdom has worked at all times, and again today, for the well-being of all people.

With an additional DVD, go with Gabriele, the prophetess and messenger of God for our time, on a walk over the land of peace. See what has been transformed by her from the seven-dimensional world into our three dimensions, and all that has developed. And hear what contemporaries, who know Gabriele, have to say about her.

284 pages / Order No. S 456en, ISBN: 978-1-890841-67-6
Color Illustrated, with DVD

The Message from the All –
The Prophecy of God Today - Not the Word of the Bible
Volume 1

God does not forsake humankind, His children. He again speaks His direct word through His prophetess and gives answers to the basic questions of mankind, particularly in relation to the spiritual correlations that are not explained in the Bible: on the meaning and purpose of the earthly life, on the freedom of every being, on cause and effect, on the imortal sould and reincarnation, on the deed of redemption of Christ, on the infinite love of God for every person and for all of creation, and much, much more.

For over 30 years, the All-Spirit, GOD, has been giving humankind His word in countless revelations through Gabriele, His prophetess and messenger. From the great treasure of these divine revelations, 14 have been selected and are now published for the first time in this volume.

The light of the eternal truth shines into our time and into the events of our time, so that each one, who opens his heart to the message of God, may recognize what God has to say to him, and, if he wants to, apply it in his life.

187 pages / Order No. S 137en, ISBN: 978-1-890841-36-2

The Path to Cosmic Consciousness –
Happiness, Freedom and Peace

The path to cosmic consciousness is the path to inner happiness and inner peace, to the feeling of having "arrived." Where? In the Kingdom of God, of which Jesus, the Christ, already taught, that it can be found within, in every person. It is our true, divine being. This is a path of liberation, which Gabriele, the prophetess and messenger of God, walked ahead of us. As a guide, she showed how we can learn not only to fulfill our work more quickly and conscientiously, but also how we can make peace with our fellowman and with nature and the animals, and how we can maintain it. Through this, we become happy and free!

75 pages / Order No. S 341en, ISBN: 978-1-890841-60-7

Your Child and You

Every soul comes into this world with different capabilities, talents and qualities, but also with different soul burdens and base human tendencies and emotions. If these qualities, talents and capabilities of the soul as well as what it lack are recognized in time, then the positive can be supported and the unlawful corrected in time.

An invaluable book for raising babies and small children in the right way. With ground-breaking knowledge about spiritual correlations and many specific instructions for the every day practical questions a new mother is confronted with.

108 pages / Order No. S 110en, ISBN: 978-1-890841-62-1

Liobani – I Explain – Will You Join Me?

Liobani helps young people find freedom in God and take their life into their hands: How do I find out what my type is and what my abilities are? What is the right profession for me? How do I deal with difficult situations involving my parents or friend? Love at first sight? ... From the contents: The Basis for a Good Relationship - Our Attitude Toward Work and Income - The Consciousness in You, the Inner Helper and Advisor - Find the Truth - There Are No Coincidences - The Free Will ...

206 pages / Order No. S 130en, ISBN: 978-1-890841-66-9

Everyone Dies for Himself Alone
Living and Dying in Order to Keep Living

For everyone who wants to find their way out of the fear of death and into a conscious life that bears in itself a sense of security, equanimity and inner stability; because as Gabriele writes: "Whoever learns to understand his life, will no longer fear death." She extensively informs us, among other things, about until now unknown correlations between life and death, about the condition and state of the soul during the whole process of dying in all the different situations it faces, and what awaits the soul of a person "over there," in the beyond, after the demise of its physical body.

144 pages / Order No. S 368en, ISBN: 978-1-890841-35-5

Cause and Development of All Illness
What a person sows, he will reap

A book more relevant than ever before, more exciting than a thriller, more moving than a documentary ... Many details revealed over 25 years ago by the Spirit of God are confirmed today by science: Without a healthy, balanced relationship between human beings, animals, plants and minerals, mankind will not survive in the long run. What does this mean for the future? What are the effects of man's destructive behavior toward nature, the animals and, not least, his own state of health?

Learn about until now unknown correlations and frontier zones between spirit and matter, about the effect of the power of thoughts on our life, for instance, how harmful parasites and pathogens can be created by our behavior patterns, about holistic healing, the meaning of life on earth, and much more ...

360 pages / Order No. S 117en, ISBN: 978-1-890841-37-9

Life with our Animal Brothers and Sisters
You, the Animal – You, the Human Being

An unusual book on animals that explains the emergence of the life forms of nature and the all-encompassing, effective and fundamental spiritual principles governing all of life. We learn about the communication between animals and nature beings, the possibility for people to communicate with animals, why animals attack us, the right way of treating them, and much more.

108 pages / Order No. S 133en, ISBN: 978-1-890841-25-6

The Animal-Friendly Cookbook

Over the course of a lifetime, a person can save the lives of 450 animals, simply by not eating meat. This alone gives good reason to become vegetarian, or vegan! The bonus? You remain healthy and fit! This book is meant to serve all who want to contribute less and less to our world's environmental problems, to suffering in slaughterhouses and inhumane conditions in factory farming.

208 pages / High-gloss color illustr. / Order No. S 436en

The Sermon on the Mount –
Life in Accordance With the Law of God

Timeless instructions for a peaceful and fulfilled life. A path that leads the way out of the dead-end in which so many people find themselves today. An excerpt from a work of revelation "This Is My Word."

112 pages / Order No. S 008en, ISBN: 978-1-890841-42-3

Live the Moment –
and You Will See and Recognize Yourself

Now, in this instant, the state of our soul shows itself. We can see it in our feelings, thoughts, words and actions that take place at every moment in us. Become sensitive to the signals of your inner life...

76 pages / Order No. S 315en, ISBN: 978-1-890841-54-6

God Heals

There is a mighty, indescribable power in us. It is the central power of love, God's power and healing. Learn how this power in you can be unfolded!

61 pages / Order No. S 309en, ISBN: 978-1-890841-23-2

For a free catalog of our books, please contact:

The Word – The Universal Spirit

P.O. Box 3549
Woodbridge, CT 06525
USA

P.O. Box 5643
97006 Würzburg
Germany

1-800-846-2691 / www.Universal-Spirit.org